GOD DOESN'T DO FOCUS GROUPS

WHY WE EXPERIENCE UNFULFILLED EXPECTATIONS IN OUR WALK WITH THE LORD

JOHN VAN VEEN

VIDE

Vide Press
6200 Second Street
Washington D.C. 20011
www.VidePress.com

ISBN: 978-1-954618-08-4 (Print)
ISBN: 978-1-954618-09-1 (ebook)

Printed in the United States of America

Cover by Miblart.com

Scripture quotations are from The ESV® Bible (The Holy Bible, English Standard Version®), copyright © 2001 by Crossway, a publishing ministry of Good News Publishers. Used by permission. All rights reserved.

Introduction

Back in the day, I was fortunate enough to work for one of the largest companies in America. It was multinational, reaching from one end of the globe to the other.

I served most of my career in the logistics arm, but also had brief stints in manufacturing. Early on in my career, I thought, as most young professionals do, that what I did was *the* most important task not just at the site I worked, but for the entire company. Consequently, when I proposed a project that could have improved the flow of things and the funding was rejected, I was a little miffed.

Naturally, I would seek out my boss: "What the heck happened? Why is this project not being funded?"

That is when I was told the *purpose* of this company. "We are not a manufacturing company. We are a *marketing* company," came the succinct reply.

He went on to explain that we make products almost as a sidelight to the development and marketing of those products. He polished off my educational moment by declaring, "Truth be told, the company would likely prefer to be *only* a marketing company."

Soundly defeated and brusquely put in my place, I walked away still miffed, but also, intrigued. Could a company really succeed without making anything, but simply by marketing it? The possibility of this had never crossed my mind, but when it did, I was captivated by the possibilities.

In future assignments, I was privileged to work more closely with the product development, sales, and marketing arms of this company–great people, full of energy, enthusiasm, and *ideas*. Many of the ideas generated by these groups would never get off the ground, but, to a marketing company, that is perfectly okay.

It was in the generation of ideas that breakthrough products were often surfaced.

Each idea that was devised went through several phases of evaluation. It started small, but for each gate this idea passed, more people would get involved. If it appeared this idea would sell on the market, the company would do a couple of things simultaneously.

First, they would try to find out how to mass produce the item. To assess this, they would send the proposed design and technical specifications to the manufacturing site allowing them time to figure out how to tweak the machinery to make the product. From this step, we would get a workable range of costs associated with the production of the product.

At the same time, we would take the nearly refined product to a group of people "off the street" and solicit input and feedback on the nature of this item. We would let them use the product, test it, and even try to break it. From their experience, we would ask them a bevy of questions, like: "What did you like about it? What surprised you? What is one thing that should be changed to improve performance and/or quality?" Questions like this, as well as watching their reactions to using the item, were foundational to driving a product idea that would succeed in the marketplace.

This process is called "Focus Group".

Focus groups are used to *improve* a product. To garner systemic input from a relevant user group and use their input to change the product to enhance the likelihood of its success once it gets rolled out. It allows for refining the innovation of the product being brought into existence. Our marketing company relied heavily on this technique as one of the final steps before deciding to launch the idea, or to shelve it. It was the "last gate" to pass.

The participants in the focus group are used to finalize the item. Their input is used to modify both the item and its packaging to make the item more useful, more attractive, more effective, and more appealing. Focus groups can also help when coming up with a price point for the item.

Even though the company owned the idea and the physical form it would take, we trusted these users to reshape it to make it easier to use, more efficient, and more flexible for the end user. This helps to improve the probability that this product would *succeed* in the marketplace.

Why is this important?

Well, as God began to reshape my understanding of my purpose in His kingdom, I left this company and went into the ministry, pastoring a church in rural North Carolina. It was in this late-in-life role that I ran, completely unexpectedly, into this very same evaluative method I had come to appreciate from the private sector. This time it was applied to a curious end.

Often, I discovered, "we", and by that I mean God-fearing people, take this technique of evaluating how to improve something, and bring it into how we relate to our God. It has worked so well in the business world, and certainly *should* work in this arena of faith and spiritual development.

Granted, much of this is not consciously derived. Meaning, few, if any of those involved would ever define what they were engaged in as a "focus group" with God, even if that is really what was happening. It exists within us, even those who would profess submission to Jesus, to demand that God seek our input into matters of faith because we, of course, have great ideas on how to improve what He designed.

He *needs* to listen to us, is the assertion I kept hearing, again not so much through vocalized words, but clearly through actions, attitudes, and intentions. Through *many* such experiences, coupled with struggling with this in my own faith journey, and in those I was attending and shepherding, the constant variable was suggesting that God modify, reduce, or replace *some* of what He had previously declared as "righteous and good".

The second constant variable of all of this was, predictably, the rejection by God of our input. And it is painful for us to repeatedly learn, *God does not do focus groups!*

He is *not* at all interested in our opinion as to how His religious process of faith, righteousness, and salvation could be improved, or be made more user friendly or be more attractive to more people.

Most of us, though, do not like taking "no" for an answer. Not even from God. So, we keep pressing Him to embrace *our* great innovations of His process.

Certainly, we maintain that if God would only modify this, or relax that, or eliminate something else, *more* people would then "use" His religious process. Wouldn't that be a good thing?

"God are You listening? We have much needed input to *help* You keep *Your* religious and spiritual commands vibrant and relevant. Isn't that what You'd want?"

Now, I want to be clear: this is not *new* to this generation. It is not even new to the "last days" age we are living in. No, we can find evidence of "God You *must* take my input seriously" all the way back to the saints of the Old Testament period.

This notion of focus groups may have gotten started with Job.

As the freedom Satan was given to introduce incredible hardship, unfathomable emotional pain, and excruciating physical distress impacted Job, Job knew all he lost and suffered was *not* from Satan but from the very hand of the God he loved. Certainly, God was making a mistake. Certainly, God, *You* need to hear me and change Your approach toward me (Job 7:20, 21).

There are, of course, many other such examples in Job's response to such unparalleled calamity. "God, if you're out there, You need to change Your methods." That is the primary objective of the focus group approach to our faith.

David, too, shared in this process of challenging God to change His methods.

"Why do the wicked prosper and the righteous go punished?" (Psalm 94:3–7). You can hear David "suggest" this is *not* how it should be done. "Listen to me, God, and know that I have much needed input to 'fix' this error on Your part. *You* should have a process that punishes evil and rewards right behavior. If You did, so many more people would rush to You." At least that appears to be how David saw it.

Jeremiah jumped on this notion David developed as he also said, "Why does the way of the wicked prosper?" (Jer 12:1), which was his question designed to get God to the table to talk about how to stop such nonsense. Much like David before him, Jeremiah saw the short-term victories of the wicked as somehow a flaw in the system God had designed. A flaw that needed to be fixed if God would *only* listen.

As you can see, this desire for mankind to demand God do a focus group is certainly not exclusive to the age we live in. It has been around a long time. At the same time, I do want to explore some of these attitudes I've seen in this age. I want to share how they are expressed and examine how God deals with them through the lens of His involvement with His people, over the centuries we see covered in the Old Testament and the decades covered by the New.

To set the basis for this, let me share an all too common experience I have had with churched people (I distinguish these from *believers* in Jesus). I have found that the "churched people", are typically people who had had a period of their lives when they were not only in church, but fairly active in religious things. Somewhere, along the way, they not only became inactive, as in from burn out, but they left the church altogether. The existence of this type of person came onto my radar through my interactions with them.

In my years as Pastor, I have had many occasions to talk with people from all walks of life, in all situations in life. From those who are "down and out" to those who are very well to do; from those who are near death's door to those who've just entered a beautiful period of life (e.g., just got married, just had a baby, or got a great promotion, etc.). In these conversations, being a pastor, a topic usually comes up, namely "faith". Normally, I pose "faith" in the context of a question, knowing many of them to be "churched". It goes something like this: "How have you seen your faith impact what you are dealing with?"

To this I get as varied a response as one can imagine. But *the* most troubling of the responses I get is this: "I've tried Jesus, He just didn't work for me."

The first couple of times this response was uttered, it absolutely stunned me. After a while, I worked to keep myself from getting numbed to this answer.

There is much I can say about this, and the horribly wrong underlying assumption over why Jesus came, but for the sake of this book, I want to submit that the meaning behind this declaration is one that says, Jesus wasn't what I expected.

Now some of that can be *bad* teaching or preaching, and sadly I have witnessed a lot of "spiritual abuse" under the guise of "preaching the Word." But much of the time, the issue lies in the organizational chart of who leads whom these folks have in their heart and mind. They see Jesus not as King of Kings worthy of our yieldedness, but as someone whose job it is to make sure *they* are well, vibrant, protected, and successful. In other words, they see Jesus as working *for* them and their agenda.

Now they *try* to make it "work with Jesus." They will do some Bible study; they will pursue answers to the questions that vex them; they will go to church routinely; and they will try to understand what Jesus asks of them.

These are not typically people who show up once a quarter and have no idea where Genesis is found. Rather, these are people who give "it" a serious go for a time. But at some point, they throw up their spiritual hands and declare Jesus to be a disappointment, not unlike other efforts they have undergone to bring order, peace, and rest into their souls–into their lives.

And here is where they seem to feel the sting of God's unwillingness to engage them in a "focus group".

They *tried* to get God to the table to talk about how to improve *their* experiences with Him. They *tried* to tell God how He could make His experience of faith and salvation more "user friendly" so they could feel like they had succeeded in matters of faith. They *tried* to tell God how their partnership with God could be improved so that they would feel listened to and valued. Of course, they found He was *very* unresponsive to their requests, so over time and multiplied frustration, the requests morphed into demands.

Once He refused the request, and then refused to budge on these demands, these churched people found God to be too inflexible; an unwilling partner that they, subsequently, divorced.

If God would only have relented and agreed to do a focus group with *me* but, instead, they found out in an exquisitely taxing way that God does not do focus groups.

From these many conversations, I have organized chapters based on the various ways we demand that God invite us into a "focus group" session to improve *our* view of His religious process.

I will look into the subtle ways we are demanding God invite us to the table, get our input, and, more importantly, buy into this great idea we have for Him. And all of these approaches are tied, I've found during discussions with these folks, to this major theme in the realm of Christian experience, namely, "I *tried* Jesus, He just didn't work for me."

Chapter 1:

A Life of Faith is Simply Too Hard

I had a refreshing conversation with a brother in Christ. As pastors we tend to get the "negative" conversations, about struggle, about discipline and about heartache. But every now and then we have these refreshing ones.

This brother in Christ was telling me he simply knew the Holy Spirit was pushing him to start tithing. This is a good thing, I told him, and we left this conversation with some joy known only to those who risk obedience. We left with real hope that God would encourage, bless, and help him in his desire to obey in this area of life that so often competes with affection for Jesus.

Several months passed before I had occasion to speak with him again. "How's it going with tithing?" was the logical question. While I was hoping to join him in celebrating God's goodness, the answer stunned me, "I gave it up. It was too hard. Everything seemed to break since I started tithing. My dishwasher, my car, even my pets. So, I just quit doing it. It was just too hard." I was anticipating celebrating what God was doing in him because of his obedience. Instead, I was stunned into silence as his words fell to the ground around me.

"It is just too hard." God I never knew You would create a process so darn hard...

Similarly, my wife and I were counseling a "Christian" couple who were at a crisis in their marriage. Since God mercifully delivered us through such a crisis, we have developed a ministry of help where we can speak into others' lives from our experience over the process. One of the things we routinely advocate is that each spouse begins their own serious pursuit of Jesus. To this end, in the "homework" portion of the session, we challenge them to pray each day and get into God's Word routinely. We believe that lasting change arises from learning to pursue Him and hear *from* Him.

After several sessions where this "homework assignment" was admittedly not done, the husband looked at us and finally declared, "I don't like reading the Bible. It just tells me of everything I am not doing correctly. So, I find myself at greater peace if I don't read it."

He wanted ignorance to work for him because failure abounds when he stepped into life with faith. Failure seemed likely. He would read the Bible and find only judgment in God's challenge of his personal need to change. And rather than admit *no one* is good enough, he chose to step away from a life of obedience to avoid a pervading sense of failure. It was simply too hard to work out his life in a way that honored the God he said he loved.

And this is perhaps the most tried means of getting God to the table so "we" can have a focus group.

What God is asking, we declare, is simply too hard. We cannot do it, or we do not see ourselves succeeding in doing what He asks, certainly not in an ongoing, lifelong commitment. Therefore, we try to insist that *He* change something, anything and a lot of things so that following Him is easier on us.

Jesus is very aware of this tendency within those in His creation. We see in Luke 14:12–24 that He was dealing with a group of people that were questioning why anyone would get excluded from the "great banquet" that He used as a parable to get them to see what the "price of entry" to His kingdom truly is. From here, the crowds gather and His address to them gets at the COST of discipleship, the reality, then, that the life of faith can and will often be a hard one, certainly a costly one.

He starts by saying, "If anyone comes to Me and does not hate his own father and mother and wife and children yes and even his own life, he cannot be My disciple." Paints a picture of one tough standard. Now, this is not some whacked-out pastor saying this. This is not some dude tripping on bad mushrooms. No, this is Jesus Himself establishing the expectations around discipleship.

To drive the point home, Jesus goes to everyday experiences. He talks of "what man desiring to build a tower does not first sit down and count the cost, whether he has enough to complete it?" That is the point. Jesus never hid the demands of being a disciple. It can be hard. It can leave us like David, wondering why we seem to get the short end of the deal.

But Jesus NEVER asked us to do it alone. His promise to supply *all* our needs starts, when He promised the Holy Spirit. The Spirit of the risen Christ operating in our hearts to guide us in all truth (John 16:13), to teach us (John 14:27), to enable us to rise up to the challenges that come to us (Rom 7:6), who gives us *gifts* and capabilities (Rom 14; I Corin 14) specific to the tasks we face. He shares with us the power of Jesus (Rom 8). *That* is often why *we* fail. We are trying to do *for* Jesus what He can only do *in* us. Our demand for a focus group is but one way of saying, "I can do this *without* Your help *if* You would just change a few things." When we realize that He will not change, and when we find we cannot succeed on His terms, most of the "churched" will say, "It is simply too hard."

God, You wouldn't listen to my input, therefore, I can say, "I tried You, but You didn't work for me."

Questions:

1) Which of the examples summarizes your approach to trying to get God to agree with how you want righteousness and salvation to come about?

2) Where have you found frustration in trying to do *for* Jesus rather than letting Him do *through* you?

3) What can you do to see that God's plan for you requires the cross, requires faith, and requires obedience?

4) How are you leaning into the Holy Spirit of the risen Jesus to enable you to live out His demands with joy and peace?

Chapter 2:

God's Design is out of touch with Humanity

As I said in the preface, *much* of how I came to this thesis is born from the many interactions I've had with "believers" over the many years I've been either their Sunday School leader, their pastor, or their counselor. The examples I share reveal the motivations and the demands that God change what He is asking of us. We *want* input. We *demand* input. And in this chapter, we look at perhaps the second biggest reason "Christians" end up rejecting God. This is because He simply will not invite them to shape His process and procedures.

A couple approached me and my wife for pre-marriage counseling. They were living together even as both would have declared themselves to be "born-again Christians". As our process is, we asked them to separate for the duration of the pre-marriage counseling and until the wedding itself. Of course, when this "line" of sexual intimacy has been crossed and the two have moved in together, it is extremely taxing to step back away from it. All the interdependencies have been established not to mention the financial implications of having "two households" again. It is *hard* to contemplate, but we firmly believe it is an act of obedience to God's standard.

One person of the couple, clearly deeply troubled by the request made of them, went to a beloved relative, someone who was attending the same church I was at the time. When the request was shared with this person, the answer was quite revealing: "Oh, it's OK if you keep living together. It will be too hard on you and God won't mind because everyone's doing it."

This from a professed believer. "God won't mind. Everyone is doing it."

What this answer, the sentiment behind it, is getting at is that God is out of touch with what is going on in our ever-increasing enlightenment as humans, as a society. Consequently, the assertion becomes: God certainly does not insist on enforcing His standard when our culture is saying, "it is OK," and especially when even our trusted spiritual mentors are saying, "it is OK."

To this end, we assert that God needs to invite us to the table to talk about how to incorporate social norms into His processes of righteousness and salvation. What may have worked centuries before, clearly no longer reflects what is in the best interest of humans as they strive to reach their full potential, their "idealized self". God needs to listen and come alongside our efforts to reach new depths of our emotional and intellectual evolution.

What this portends, though, is an assault on biblical norms.

This is more true in the Western world than elsewhere, but it is only a matter of time for the "elsewhere" to experience the same pressure to acquiesce to the enlightened thesis. Western society has deemed biblical values of fidelity, one-man-one-woman relationships, and the sanctity of human life to be "restrictive, punitive, and demeaning".

Society has told us all that God is clearly out of touch with the evolution of human wisdom, philosophy, and theology. We are right to think that our way of thinking is correct, and if that brings us into conflict with God, then *He* has the problem. Then *He* is in need of change. And if He would invite us to the table, we could clearly help Him make the necessary adjustments that would serve to improve His "product" and, in that, His reputation in this increasingly enlightened world of ours.

Now, that is not to say the folks in this persuasion of people will never find a good use for God. They will and often do. For example, when what God says reinforces their preferred message track then they embrace Him. When God says, as He does, *love* everyone, stop racist, classist, sexist behaviors and serve the poor, then, to these folks, God is now "right on" and should be given a shout out. But when He insists on things where we have taken a different position, then God is declared to be intolerant, and a bigot who fuels hatred. What we see in all of this is a group of so-called Christians who see the Gospel as something that works for *their* agenda and only when that happens, are they "good with God".

But God is unwilling to yield.

He insists His entire counsel be embraced. He is not interested in providing us a "buffet" of ideas that we pick and choose from. Rather, Jesus said, "He who *keeps* My commandments is he that Father loves," (John 14:21). Consequently, when people disposed to say God is out of touch rush repeatedly headlong into His *complete* instruction on a righteous life, they often quit Jesus altogether, again, because "he didn't work for me."

Clearly, this is not His way. He is not someone who works *for* us. Rather, as we saw in Chapter 1, His demands of us are extreme. He insists on us embracing *all* of His Word. As He lodged His complaint against the church in Laodicea (Rev 3:15), "I *know* your works, you are neither hot nor cold. Would that you were either hot or cold. So, because you are lukewarm and neither hot nor cold, I will spit you out of my mouth..." His message was one of this church being sold out, not to Christ, but to other systems of belief that had this "church" embrace His Word in a very noncommittal way. The idea here is they picked and chose what to embrace and what to ignore, largely driven by what society had deemed permissible and worthy of celebration.

That is not God's design for those who call Him Savior.

As Paul told the Romans, (Rom 1:21), "Although they knew God, they did not honor Him as God..." That is the essence of this demand for God to be more flexible. Paul adds, they "became futile in their thinking and since they did not see fit to acknowledge God, God gave them up to a debased mind to do what ought not to be done." (Rom 1:21,28). There is the solution. This demand for a focus group sourced in our insistence that God become as "enlightened" as we've become actually has as its root the denial of God outright.

Therefore, the solution to this reason that God should have a focus group is to get back to realizing that God is a God of order, that *He* chose to create this world. *He* chose to create human beings and as a result *He* knows what is best for us. The created thing never sees itself accurately. Only the creator of the "thing" does.

In this way, while the Bible is many things, one thing it is for sure is a handbook on how to live life as God always intended for it to be lived.

He loved us so much He overlooks our sin for those who believe in the person and work of Jesus Christ. He loved us so much He gave us the Eternal Word Who brought us words that were spoken in heaven to this earth. He loved us so much He made Himself fully known to us. As Wayne Grudem has said, "God has caused to be recorded in Scripture everything that we need to know about

Jesus' words and deeds in order to trust and obey Him perfectly."
(*Systematic Theology* p. 132).

We cannot pick and choose, like we were at some spiritual
Golden Corral. His entire Word is to be embraced, even when
understanding parts of it can be perplexing. Society cannot declare
some precepts of Jesus no longer applicable. We are called to "keep
My commandments" and to "hold fast to the profession of faith"
(Heb 4:14). Doing so will keep us from being "a wave of the sea
that is driven and tossed about by the wind" (James 1:6). The
challenge in this case is to be "doers of the Word, not hearers only"
(James 1:22) for "the one who looks into the perfect law, the law of
liberty and perseveres, being no hearer who forgets but a doer who
acts, he will be blessed in his doing." (James 1:25).

God is *not* out of touch with humanity. He understands it *far* better
than humans can, will, or do.

Questions:

1) In what arena of societal enlightenment are you most likely to
find yourself agreeing with the position of those who want to
pick and choose what is truth, and its arguments?

2) If you had to rate your study habits as it relates to God's Word,
what grade would you give yourself for **effort** and **competence**
in handling His word?

3) Where do you experience being "tossed around" in your
spiritual beliefs?

4) What keeps you from embracing the full counsel of God for
how you are to live?

Chapter 3:

God does not address the needs in Society

Throughout the Bible, we often see God bringing our attention to truth that unsettles us. OK. He did that on a LOT of things.

But in this case where we're dealing with issues in society, Matt 26:11, Jesus said, "The poor you will always have with you." And He said this on the heels of His challenge to care for the "least of these" (Matt 25: 34-40), so it is not like the notion of poverty was far from Him when He spoke this axiom. But we call on God to account for the injustices in this world. We want Him to come to the table to talk about how to improve the performance of *His* system that seems to, in many minds, foster injustice. So, the demand here, for this focus group effort is people want a gospel that eliminates social injustices and all the "-isms" *we* put on each other. You know, classism, racism, sexism, etc.

From this "demand" of God for a focus group, we have seen the rise of the Social Justice Gospel. I had one pastor tell me he does not "believe anyone is saved *unless* they serve the poor". That is the crux of the issue they have with God. And there are verses that point to caring for the least of these, as referenced above, so to *some* extent, he was not stating something the Bible declared as irrelevant. The issue, though, becomes erroneous when the underlying assertion is salvation equals social justice.

The prevailing opinion of this "gospel" is that God is not doing what He should to eliminate injustice, to eliminate inequity, to eliminate poverty, and to eliminate the deep psychological impacts of abused people. Therefore, people rise up and insist that the priority of the church be dealing with injustice and inequality.

To be fair, some of what these church leaders have done has added value by creating necessary dialogue around these topics so vital to living with "no distinctions," as I will share in a little bit. However, by and large they find that God is not clear enough for their liking on topics that often dominate the headlines which tend to lead them to dominate our emotional spirits as well. In this, they then work to dictate to us what is "fair and unfair". This is where they demand God invite them to the table to upgrade His stated positions on these explosive issues within society.

For example, God nowhere declares being wealthy as a sin. The *love* of money is clearly called out, but not simply having money (1 Tim 6:10). There are those that say, "You have too much money, so you should be forced to give more to the poor." Because God's Word contains no such commandments, He *needs* a focus group around such issues which obviously contribute to discrimination, class struggles, and even crime.

Finally, for a topic so explosive, there is nowhere in His Word where God declares any race being the specific cause of detestable practices. Given the horrific events of May 25, 2020, there have been many who have been outspoken in asserting that if "you are a white person, you are a racist". We have as a society begun to insist white privilege is so much the cause of inequality, injustice, and poverty. Yet, God never assigns a race of people as "the issue" in our collective shortcomings. He does, though, clearly name what is, in fact, the issue in our collective shortcomings. He calls it "sin" and He declares this deep seated darkness is within *everyone*.

However, it is much easier for us if we can assign blame. Consequently, we give God our input on the cause *and* the solution. We tell Him what He has designed in His Word, what He has shared through His wisdom is simply not sufficient to deal with these dark maladies that plague mankind and stifle society. Therefore, man then steps in, and begins to insist on standards of salvation that the Bible does not teach/hold. They begin to insist that there are "new sins" that need to be called out. They begin to assert that the only real gospel is the one that helps the poor, that deals with the "-isms," and that addresses injustice. Anything besides this focus is, in this system of belief, unnecessary and distracting and clearly *not* what God should be endorsing.

It is a false gospel. It lessens the work of Jesus. It elevates the ideas of man.

Yes, we *are* called to consider everyone as equal, as image-bearers, and to hold *no* distinction (Col 3:11 and Gal 3:28) among people groups. Unity, as Jesus prayed in John 17, is *the* hallmark of those who truly love, obey, and honor Him. We are called, in this regard, to "put on compassionate hearts, kindness, humility, meekness and patience" (Col 3:14) as His means for ensuring that we draw no distinctions among people. This means we are to consciously, intentionally, fight against those judgments that well up within us, and refuse to give them a voice *in* us. We are to reject these types of instinctive reactions and walk to the closet and pick out *His* clothes and put them on. We are to wear them for our sake, but also for the sake of those of whom we may naturally want to draw distinctions around.

The Gospel is one of peace, but also one of order and process change. Yes, "revolution" *can* happen–meaning God changes things instantly, miraculously, and completely. My experience, though, in the vast majority of time, God deals with us through what I call "evolution", meaning slow change occurring over longer periods of time.

These needs in society that seem to scream that God is in need of our input at His next focus group meeting are *not* national outages, or international outages. They are *individual* outages that stem from the heart of each individual person.

Jesus said, "Out of what abides in and overflows from the heart, the mouth speaks" (Matt 12:34). It is what is horribly wrong *within* mankind that these distinctions are not only drawn, but acted upon in the most heinous of ways. God rightly spoke through Jeremiah when He said, "The heart is deceitful above all things and who can understand it" (Jer 17:9).

God *knows* the issue is not one of the Bible being immaterial to the solution of what ills society. God knows His Word is *the only* solution to the ills of society. But because man sees it differently, we insist God bend to our understanding. We insist God take our input and change His approach and His demands. How ironic, then, that we blame God for not caring when He has offered *the* answer to all of this repentance and faith in Jesus Christ so that our heart of selfish, divisive hate can be replaced with selfless, loving embrace.

Questions:

1) Where have you been guilty of presuming God's Word to be insufficient to handle the complexities of the ills in society today?

2) How has this impacted the quality of your faith and trust in the Lord?

3) In what areas of your life has God produced revolutionary change? Evolutionary change? Why the difference in His approach do you suppose?

4) How can you be an agent of true change in these unmistakable needs within society?

Chapter 4:

You really want me to suffer for the sake of the Gospel?

We live in a period of "church history" where we have been told we are "King's Kids" and, as such, we should have the richness of being a "kid of the King". We have been told that God wants us to have the best parking spot in the shopping center. We have been told that God will give back to you tenfold of what you give to Him. We have been told that God truly wants us to be happy.

It is no wonder then that when suffering comes, for the sake of His name, that *we* get horribly disoriented. If God wants all these great things for me, why am I being opposed? Why have I lost my job? Why is my daughter sick? We have lost the biblical perspective that we *are* strangers on this earth and have grown way too comfortable seeking comfort, and worse, insisting that it is God's job to provide and then protect our personal comfort.

One Sunday I was sharing from a text in Acts (Acts 13:1–3) concerning how the Holy Spirit called Paul and Barnabas to the mission field. It reads, "Now there were in the church at Antioch prophets and teachers while they were worshiping the Lord and fasting, the Holy Spirit said, 'set apart for me Barnabas and Saul for the work to which I have called them.'". These two pillars of the early church were *not* seeking to go, but the Holy Spirit made it *very* clear they were to go.

So, naturally I asked how our church would like to see a similar call today? Later, one member said, "I don't want my kids anywhere near the mission field. They need to stay home, and stay close where it is safe." The risk of suffering was too great. The gospel would simply have to advance without help from "us".

Generally, these are people who see the gospel as either not all that important, or as a way to make their lives easier. They see devotion to Jesus as some kind of talisman that protects, insulates, and elevates their state as well as their status in life. But they are not really sold out to His Great Commission, because personal comfort is more necessary. Similarly, they see Jesus as working *for* them, with His job being their personal advancement, without any real commitment on their part to be commended by Jesus. Finally, they believe that Jesus comes in a bottle and all one needs to do is rub it and claim another promise of which Jesus owes us the fulfillment. All this without a real concern that we are commanded to go, commanded to risk our own comfort.

I have a friend who is of a denominational persuasion that insists you can call down healing from heaven, that God does not want any of His children sick. Therefore, if you are sick, one of two things are happening. Either you are not His child to begin with or you do not have the faith to be made well. See, in this system of belief, there is simply no room for personal suffering. That is not a part of the "deal" God makes with us when we consent to being saved, at least that is how this is viewed through the lens of such people.

People in this camp of "faith" see suffering as something done in remote parts of this world and that God certainly does not see

such abuse as necessary here in the spiritually enlightened parts
of the world. As if to say suffering is beneath their higher state of
sophistication, status, and, yes, salvation. These people are insisting
that God embrace their input on the role of suffering. They see
a focus group with God and driving out this unwanted trait often
associated with Christlikeness. They see the gospel as a tool that
gives them everything they could want from a religious experience
but is also a tool that should never ask anything of them.

This, too, is a false gospel. Suffering is somewhere along the path
of every person who truly lives out the claims of God on their lives.
It may not be death, but it will be something, even many things
for the Bible serves to warn us of such treatment by the forces that
oppose the Gospel of Jesus Christ.

God does not hide the reality of suffering from us, as if when it
happens we are caught completely unaware. No, rather He has
routinely warned us that there will be times of trouble. Jesus
Himself rightly stated, "In this world you WILL have trouble, but
take heart, I have overcome the world" (John 16:33).

In His great prayer on behalf of those who truly believe in His
name, Jesus said, "I have given them Your word and the world has
hated them because they are not of the world, just as I am not of
this world" (John 17:14).

Certainly, there is much more to this truth than suffer for the gospel
we must. Paul, in 2 Corin 11, summarizes the fulfillment of the
Word spoken over him to Ananias, when he was very reluctant to
seek out who was then Saul per the Lord's request.

Acts 9:16 reads, "For I will show him how much he must suffer for
the sake of My name." In his summary, Paul lists being flogged,
beaten with rods, stoned and left for dead as but *some* of the events
that came to him *solely* because of the Gospel of Jesus Christ. He
concluded, from all of his personal experiences with suffering. "For

the sake of Christ, I am content with weaknesses, insults, hardships, persecutions and calamities. For when I am weak, then I am strong." (2 Cor 12:10).

Paul called all he endured, "light momentary affliction" (2 Cor 4:17). Now, I recognize most, if not all of us, *hope* we do not have to suffer. No one relishes in such rejection and pain and loss. But those in Christ, understand it is a part of the journey. *It* comes with being, as the writer said of Abraham, a "stranger in a strange land looking for a city whose architect and builder is God" (Heb 11:9,10).

Suffering, in Christ, has multiple sources, multiple purposes.

Sometimes suffering is "discipline" as the writer of Hebrews shared (Heb 12:5–8). It is part of God's teaching tools to help us better grasp what stands in the way of us experiencing a richer life in Christ. It is a necessary aspect of teaching us how to let go of what is false and learn to trust in Him. We understand being disciplined and why it is valuable to us.

Sometimes suffering is Satan's designed attack on us targeting our resolve and trying to weaken it so that we might quit following Jesus. It comes as hostility against us (Heb 12:3). It comes as sickness and injury in us (Job 2). It comes as economic and emotional loss (Job 1). It comes as a physical attack against us (Acts 8). Suffering comes. Even when Satan seems to be its author, we also know God uses all things to work together for our good (Rom 8:28). Finally, suffering is a part of how God chooses to refine us so that we are more accurate image-bearers of His Son (Rev 2:8–11).

All this being true, the Lord gives us the whole equation of which suffering is but one part.

Suffering is not solely about loss. Even as Paul, considered all he endured as "momentary light affliction," he was able to do so because Jesus showed him the *benefit* tied to enduring suffering. "For this light momentary affliction is preparing for us an eternal weight of glory beyond all comparison" (2 Cor 4:17).

Suffering was necessary, and he willingly underwent it because Jesus showed him what was waiting a glory so rich, full, and weighty that he could see these things that torture us on earth as being what they were. In view of eternity, they are momentary and light.

Of course, Jesus, as Isaiah prophesied, was well acquainted with grief, was a man of sorrow, smitten for our sake (Is 53:3–5). Jesus *knew* suffering. If no other time, and there were plenty of other times, than during Passion Week, where His passion to do the Father's will drove Him to endure such brutality, suffering of unimagined proportion. "Who for the joy that was set before Him endured the cross, despising the shame and is seated at the right hand of the throne of God" (Heb 12:2).

There is joy in Christ that puts suffering in its rightful place. It is this joy that gives us a whole different perspective on suffering.

Questions:

1) Are you living as if suffering is optional? That Jesus really does not want that path for you? How might this change your reflections on this?

2) How have you suffered for Christ? How did this compare to the benefit you received for enduring it?

3) Given the counsel of God on this topic, how might you prepare yourself for the future events of suffering?

4) What does God say about the role of suffering, to you?

Chapter 5:

It is Unfair that some people are Excluded from Heaven

This phenomenon has been around for quite some time.

It is born in what I call the "equity gospel" that establishes "sincerity" and "innate goodness" as the requirements for heaven. It sounds like, "Well, I wouldn't want to serve a God that sends people to hell." It expresses a demand that God come to the table, invoke a focus group, so we can right this wrong in God's theology. It is where the recent notion of "Love Wins" is born. If God is a God of love, then surely He wants everyone in Heaven. We will help Him see that this is only good and right.

In dealing, generally, with those who do not know Jesus, this is perhaps the "go to" argument for why they are choosing to ignore the gospel. I was sharing the gospel with a younger man, perhaps in his mid-20s. He was polite. He listened respectfully and did not take an aggressive, hostile posture. But when I asked him what he thought about why Jesus came to Earth, his answer almost seemed a "stock one" which ignored my question entirely.

"Well," he replied. "I'm not sure I can serve a God who sends people to hell simply because they choose to believe in some other god."

He was not arguing with the fact that he needed forgiveness, that there was a sense of justice due him. He was not upset that God was demanding accountability for his shortcomings. No, his sole issue was that people were being excluded from Heaven because they would not, or could not, acknowledge what Jesus had done for them. Consequently, "good people I know, according to you, won't go to Heaven because they refuse to do it this way. That is just not right, nor fair. And I can't get into a god who does that."

By implication: "God are you listening to me? Do you see how what You designed is in error and can be fixed by adopting my input?"

Some of this "need" to have a broader inclusion into Heaven is to avoid the reality of there being an alternative eternal site to Heaven. Yes, the biblical claim to a "Hell" also drives people to question that God is "loving". They posit the question: "How can a God who claims to *love* then turn around and send them to such a horrible place?" The possibility of such a place has also led former thought leaders in "Christianity" to "change their mind" on what God would claim to be true. Hell is simply too heinous to be considered a real "home". A loving God cannot do that. Hell does not exist.

For a place that *we* declare does not exist, Jesus sure talked of it a lot. Whether that be in the Gospels or in the final Revelation of grace to John on Patmos, Jesus was very clear that there is a place of eternal torment reserved for those who despise the Son, His claims, and His work.

Jesus, in a parable explains how those that seek to injure the work of the Kingdom will be treated. He mentioned that the "Son of Man (i.e., Jesus) will send His angels and they will gather out of His kingdom all causes of sin and all law-breakers and throw them into the fiery furnace." (Matt 13:41, 42).

Again, in the parable of the Great Wedding Feast, Jesus explained that one needs to be invited to His marriage supper *and* wear clothes that He provided in order to be seated with Him in this celebration. For those that tried to squeeze in on their own terms, Jesus said "bind (them) and cast (them) into outer darkness. In that place there will be weeping and gnashing of teeth."

One more reference. Jesus, looking at "the final judgment" in Matthew 25, declares that the "goats will go away into eternal punishment, but the righteous into eternal life." Jesus was very clear that there is a place of eternal punishment even as there is a place of eternal life. Hell is real. Heaven is real. And in Matt 25, Jesus is equally clear that Heaven is a place of reward for those that welcome, visit, clothe, and give in His name to those who need.

Those committed to this notion of an "equity gospel", are trying to demand that God engage them in a focus group so they can assert their want of how people get to Heaven and how to eliminate the biblical reality of a place of eternal suffering. God needs to listen to us on this point, or else....

Questions:

1) How narrow do you see the road to heaven? As Jesus described, or a bit wider? Why?

2) In what ways have you begun to accept that "sincerity" is the way to Heaven?

3) How do you see the existence of Hell? What role does it play in the Bible?

4) How do you know you will be in Heaven? How does that knowledge jive with what the Bible declares the "way" to be?

Chapter 6:

The Gospel is too exclusive

This issue is the close cousin of what we talked about in Chapter 5. Remember the issue in the last chapter was about people who simply cannot buy that "good people are excluded from Heaven because they didn't go at it in God's way."

The issue in this chapter takes exception with the Bible's claim that there is, in fact, but one way to Heaven Jesus said it in John 14:6, "I am THE way, the truth, and the life. NO one comes to the Father but by Me."

This statement is seen as simply arrogant and needlessly preclusive. By insisting there is only *one* way to God, people see this as intolerant and demanding and, therefore, unnecessarily exclusive.

One leader of the Prosperity Gospel once said that he "believes Buddhists and Hindus will be in heaven too, because they are so sincere in their faith." This is a common way to step around what the Bible has declared to be true. We insist that God see the issue *our* way. We value sincerity of belief even if that belief could not be more diametrically opposed to what the Bible declares. We want

God to hear us on this, to incorporate our input into His updated version of the salvation process.

In a summary, people who hold this belief are people who see the gospel as being a tool, not a requirement.

They see the gospel as relevant, valid, and necessary but only for those who so choose to access God. They see other paths as viable, too, in leading a person to eternity in heaven, as long as they are sincerely pursued and humbly practiced. They want to see sincerity lead the path into Heaven, not Jesus. They insist that God modify His claims to reflect such generosity, and, in that, correct a method that no longer fits with the "modern view of inclusion".

All in all, they want God to widen the path that leads to Heaven so that there are ways to get in past Jesus, without Him being the door to the sheep's pen (John 10:9).

Biblically, of course, Jesus laid out *the* path to the Father, who is in "heaven itself" (Heb 9:24). John 14:6 was already quoted. He is not just *the* way, the wording tells us He is *the only* way. When Jesus said "NO ONE comes to the Father, but by Me," Jesus was laying out very clearly the requirement to stand in the Father's presence, to be with Him in Heaven.

Is it exclusive? Yes. Is it necessary? Yes. For without this "narrow path," none would exist. None. Do we want others to exist? Of course, because that puts *us* back in control of our destiny. That puts Christ as simply an option among others and as His death and resurrection as realistically unnecessary for our eternal salvation. All of this is our way of insisting God come to the table and accommodate our input.

To this end, the writer of the book of Hebrews has much to say. Other methods to achieve the standard that God requires (i.e., perfection) were miserable failures. The fact that the adherents to these other processes are constantly searching for a sense of being justified, that they are constantly in need of ritualistic practices to feel some relief from pending judgment, and that they are constantly looking for more ways to appease the one they believe determines their fate; all of these activities scream that these other ways are "weak and useless" (Heb 7:18).

Enter Jesus. He is the "guarantor of a better covenant" (Heb 7:22). He is the "one who is seated at the right hand of the throne of the Majesty in heaven..." (Heb 8:1). He has "obtained a ministry that is as much more excellent than the old as the covenant He mediates is better... "(Heb 8:6). He was the one "who entered once for all into the Holy places, not by means of the blood of goats and calves but by means of His own blood, thus securing an eternal redemption" (Heb 8:12).

Consequently, those who trust in Jesus for eternal redemption, "have as a sure and steadfast anchor of the soul, a hope that enters into the inner place behind the curtain where Jesus has gone as a forerunner on our behalf..."(Heb 6:19).

It is clear that our hope is in the work of Jesus. That gives those who do believe in His work, a sense of rest, peace, security, and hope. It is unshakeable for it is delivered to us *in* Him. With such a quietness of being, there is no need to demand that God accept our invitation for a focus group on this "exclusivity".

Questions:

1) What happens to your sense of peace when you believe that God needs to open the door to Heaven a bit wider so that others can get "past Jesus"?

2) How have you responded to those who claim "sincerity" is enough to force God to accept them into Heaven?

3) What is one thing you can do to ensure you believe that God is right to be so exclusive?

4) Is your life characterized by rest, peace, quietness of soul? If not, how can you address this?

Chapter 7:

Good works are sufficient

This perspective on how one gets to Heaven is one with a long, rich history. Indirectly, it got started with those who defended the Jewish system of belief.

God initially gave His chosen people, namely the Jews, the Ten Commandments, as He was preparing them to become a nation. He also gave them many rules to follow on how to live as a people set apart in the way *He* desired. All of these rules expressed God's design for their society, including government, education, interpersonal relationships, and civic responsibilities.

But from this list, those charged with working to define the "truth of what God wants", had turned His design into a somewhat predictable legalistic process. They had, by the time Jesus was born, developed an entire encyclopedic definition of "sins".

These were rooted in what the priests had agreed what God meant to say when He gave Israel the "commandments". From their lofty assessment of God's heart, a list of 613 laws were established and codified that defined "sin" in a practical sense. The priests' jobs then included ensuring purity of the follower, holding up these laws, and calling out "sin" as they saw it.

The problem, of course, emerged from focusing on just the "rule of law". What the Lord gave in love became this legalistic approach that left the heart of God in these commandments *He* initially gave them completely "void". It had gotten so bad that God grew tired of the very offerings He instituted because those leading these required sacrifices had hearts far from God (Psalm 40:6; 51:6; Hosea 6:6). The leadership of *His* house fell to believing that simply going through the motions was all it would take to please the Father.

From this, during the era of the Apocrypha, the sect of Jewish elite theologians called the Pharisees emerged. This group only believed in the Pentateuch as being "inspired". Their mission was to enforce all the "laws" to please God. These laws were codified and then shared with the faithful and enforced by their standing as legal scholars of the faith. In this way, they saw to it that God's desires were not only expressed but enforced. God needed an "enforcement arm", these people were sure of that. If people complied, they could be assured of having done enough to merit a good standing in the life hereafter.

Yes, this notion of earning one's salvation has been around a long time.

It plays to the human desire to have complete control over one's future standing in eternity. Do the right things, enough of them, and Heaven will have to accept you, or so their argument goes. This notion of saving faith is too belittling and too vague. God needs help in making the process of eternal life easier to understand and implement. Therefore, *we* need to share our ideas so God can rectify His oversight. These are people who tend to see life as a "scale".

In an article (dated August 9, 2020) in the "Christian Post", a survey of 2000 adults completed by George Barna in January 2020, in association with the Arizona Christian University Cultural Research Center, revealed the following:

"Nearly two thirds of Americans believe that having some
kind of faith is more important than the particular faith with
which someone aligns." In addition, "sixty eight percent
of those who embrace this notion (of sincerity of faith is
more important than faith in Christ) identify as Christians,
including 56% of self-described evangelicals, 62% of those
who identify as Pentecostals." Finally, "slightly over half of
Christian respondents said they believe someone can attain
salvation by 'being or doing good'".

It is a serious issue even within the traditional conservative
evangelical belief system. You can almost hear them demand God
accept their input to their use of His process.

As a pastor, I often run into this concept that these users insist God
must embrace.

I was visiting a man who had just survived a horrific accident,
whose recovery was complicated by his drug use. He was in
a coma for nearly a month. I was in the room when the doctor
explained to his parents that he would almost certainly die, that the
possibility of death was greater than the possibility of awakening
from the coma. Naturally, then, when he did awake, *everyone* was
thrilled to tears, while some claimed God had delivered a certifiable
miracle.

When he was able to talk, I asked him why he thought God would have
so miraculously saved his physical life. His answer was concerning:

"I've been saved several times, so I know what you're getting at. But
I'm better than most people even though I've made some bad mistakes."

Being saved was less important than being "better than most
people". The scales he felt tipped enough in his favor to warrant
God giving him more life on this earth. God, are you listening? You
need to consider being *good*. That is important to us, here on earth.

We had been counseling a younger couple who were in the midst of a crisis brought on by the man's extramarital affair. They declared themselves to be firm believers in Jesus.

During one session, the woman broke down in tears and mournfully cried, "We did everything right. We did not have sex before we were married. We limited our alone time. We dated with commitment to purity. We did all of this right! *So how could this happen?*"

It was a hard litany to hear. Her heart was broken because they did *enough right* to merit protection from the sin in their own hearts.

You can hear her heart: "I *have* been good enough. Why *this* of all things?"

An elderly gentleman that I had known for many years was facing death. He was *very* uncomfortable at the prospect of both dying and of the consequence to him in death.

"I don't know if I did enough good things to get into Heaven," was his painful lament.

And the sadness on his face was measurable. Even as we had talked over the years about "never good enough, that faith in the work of Jesus is how anyone gets to Heaven," I could see the depression falling and engulfing him.

He lived his entire life believing that doing enough good was good enough. The problem, of course, at this stage in his life is he saw *now* that the "bad" was foremost in his mind and he could see, as a logical consequence, the scales tipping "against him".

He now, at least instinctively if not consciously, *knew* that he was not good enough. In fear, he also realized there was no longer sufficient time to move the scales back so they would tip toward Heaven.

Being good enough is one of the ways we demand God do "focus groups". We want Him to change the entry process into Heaven by establishing that being "good enough" as sufficient for a life that "earns" Heaven. Barna's data, from above, declares this is how *we* need God to act. We somehow want to prove to God He did not make a mistake in saving us. And in that our works are good enough for that merit.

Biblically, the road to salvation is, as Paul told the Romans, *by grace alone, faith alone in Christ alone.*

Good works, while important, as James would tell us, to *show* we believe in Jesus, can *never* save us. We hate that. It tells us we have *no* control over our future state. And that is true. Only Jesus does and blessed are those that rest in the sufficiency of His work on the cross.

As we see in 1 Corinthians 1:18, the cross *is* foolishness to those perishing. It is like, "no *way* can it be that easy. I *want* to have some say in how I get saved." But to those who are being saved, it *is* the power of God unto salvation (1 Cor 1:18).

We desperately want our good works to count for something and we wave them at the Lord and demand He value them. God doesn't do focus groups. He values *His* work alone as the source of salvation. If we can come to terms with that, then we can avoid the depression, sadness, and loss we feel because we know we are never good enough! We can avoid the desperation my elderly friend faced as he became acutely aware that his life of good works now pointedly betrayed him. He knew no one could ever do enough good works to quiet the soul that was being called to soon give account.

The antidote is to see goodness biblically, that often people who fall victim to this critique are those who are trying to prove to God He was right in saving them.

In Isaiah 64:6, God declares, to the Jews that were so keen on trying to impress him with their attempts at being righteous, at being, as we would say, good enough to merit heaven, "Your righteous deeds are like a polluted garment".

Some translations say, "filthy rags". The word picture here is not about clothes that have gotten slightly soiled, but clothes that have become so soiled, they can never be made clean and therefore must only be thrown away. That is how God views our attempts to impress Him.

Goodness and righteousness are only achieved in the work of Jesus Christ. Paul said it this way, "He has now reconciled in His body of flesh by His death, in order to present you holy and blameless and above reproach before Him. (Col 1:22).

His design for a life that is holy, that, then warrants heaven, is *through* His work in "His body of the flesh by His death." Paul told us, "For in (the Gospel of Jesus Christ) the righteousness of God is revealed from faith for faith..." (Rom 1:17). It is His standard and it is revealed as the standard in Jesus and it is secured as OUR standard by faith in the work of Jesus on the cross. That is how we achieve being "good enough". Not *our* works, but His.

Questions:

1) How have you tried to impress God with your life's actions and beliefs? Have these produced peace and rest in you?

2) Are you still trying to impress God even as you might declare you are a follower of Jesus?

3) What might be clues that you are not resting in the satisfaction of your sins through the work of Jesus?

4) Have you trusted in the work of Jesus, by faith, on your behalf? If not, is now the time?

Chapter 8:

Evil is winning because God is not that loving

Ever run into this question: "If God is so good and loving, why is there so much (fill in the blank) in this world?"

Sometimes this is an appropriate question as when it comes like this, "If God is so good and loving why do children die of horrid diseases and brutality committed against them?" Sometimes the question is clearly one of insolence as in "if God is good and loving why is there injustice and hate in this world?"

The former question gets at the grief we feel when we see a helpless and innocent child being wracked by pain. The latter question gets at our arrogance for asserting that God is the author of such things, meaning *we* are not responsible for injustice and hate. *God* knows these things exist and yet He will not stop them. Therefore, *He needs our help*. Evil is winning. God cannot, consequently, be loving. If, therefore, there is to be love, we need to input and show Him how to step it up. Invite me, please, to Your next focus group so we can get this right.

I admit, there are some circumstances, as with a child battling cancer, that do cause questions of God's love and care. No sense denying this reaction, oftentimes a visceral one. We see such senselessness and can raise our hearts and, yes, sometimes our fist toward Heaven in concern over His providence and care. This is not so much what I am trying to address in this expression of our insistence that God invite us to a focus group. This type of situation gets at the sovereignty of God, the nature of His plans and the purposes in them even when the "road we are on is full of deep emotional loss."

No, rather I want to address that issue raised by many outside of Christ and, sadly, by *some* inside His Church, that seems to insist God's sole function is to *love* everyone into eternity. And when they see evidence that this is not being done, they assume, suggest, and ridicule God for being weak and ineffective. Evil is winning, so these people assess. Therefore, to them, God is not all that He says He is. That seems to be the sentiment at work in these situations.

One way this has been expressed to me is through a statement made by a teaching elder in a church we attended. It went like this, "I know God has many attributes but the single most important one is 'God is love'. *That* is the one that best defines Him."

This is our way of saying, "Yes, God I know You have many sides, but when it comes down to it, when there is a real crisis on hand, You *will* choose love over every other attribute associated with Your character." When we hold this view, we relegate His other attributes to a secondary role, relatively unimportant and always being trumped by "love", and, to complicate matters further, "love" is often *our* definition of this word.

With this, we certainly will not countenance justice, judgment, and the wrath of God, even toward sin. Love would push these things into the rear and allow rebellion to continue. With this assessment of how God *must* function, we resign God to being an elderly grandparent who just enjoys the family, but is clueless to how dysfunctional the family truly is.

We live with a hierarchy for everything we do. We have hierarchies of teams we cheer for, hierarchies of places we would eat, hierarchies of laws we will adhere to or not. So, it is no surprise then, that we have a hierarchy of sins from absolutely horrible down to no one really cares. Some denominations even categorize sin by "mortal" which means there is no forgiveness to "venial" which means these are easy to forgive. We develop our internal hierarchy of sins, too (typically to justify indulging a sin pattern or two). "Oh, *everyone* does it" is our rationale for putting something in the "too trivial to deal with". You know like lying, gossiping, cheating, and stealing.

I have already recounted the incident of the person living with their significant other, that God will not care that this is happening because "everyone is doing it." This is us saying God's love for us *must* grant us these playful indulgences. This is us saying God has to consider what *we* think sin and evil really look like and surely, lying, stealing, gossiping are NOT sins and are by no means evil not when compared with what "so and so" does God, are You listening to my incredibly valuable input here?

Another way this demand to be included in a focus group comes across is, not so much in the micro-scale, which we just discussed, but in the "macro-scale". By this I mean the events that are captured on the nightly news, these stories of international scope and frenzy. If God is loving, how can He let Ebola and COVID-19 ravage entire population groups? If God is loving, how can He let dictators sanction and commit genocide? If God is loving, how can He let natural disasters lay waste entire regions of a country?

In these situations, the assertion is that evil is winning and thereby God cannot be loving. If He would invite me to His next group session, I can help Him see what love should do. It should wipe out all forms of suffering and loss whether that comes through the hands of an evil government or through the seeming randomness of natural disasters. That is what needs to happen. *God are you listening?*

In this, we neglect the origins of such evil. It was in Eden, that idyllic place created just for mankind. Perfect in every way. Lion and lamb were best friends. The wolf and the chicken were roommates. There were no such things as thorns, thistles, and itch-causing weeds. Death had not even been thought of. Love ruled everything, all the time. The *very* attribute we now insist be solely employed.

Then something very illogical happened. At the same time, very human. *We* thought *we* could improve on what God designed. *We* thought if *we* were just like God, then EVERYTHING must have to be even better for us.

Love somehow wasn't enough. Our "parents" jumped on the invitation to improve paradise Our parents launched the demand to help God improve what He put out there.

It did not work.

Rather than improving everything, we destroyed everything. Instead of living forever, disease, death, decay, and destruction were introduced. In God's infinite capacity to love, He gave us free will. He *wanted* us to *choose* to love Him.

In the movie Indiana Jones and the Last Crusade we have a scene that sums up our actions toward God quite accurately. Forced by the antagonist, Walter Donovan, to find the Holy Grail, "the cup of Christ" because it was thought to provide eternal life to whomever drank of it, Indiana Jones finds the room. But in this room are HUNDREDS of cups all guarded by the last surviving Templar Knight. Under duress, the Templar Knight said drink from the wrong cup, and you will die. The antagonist, Walter Donovan, scans all the possibilities and gleefully holds up a cup of splendor, decorated by many jewels. "Ah yes, the cup of a king," he says as he hoists and drinks from a cup he thought worthy of the Holy Grail. But he chose the wrong cup and immediately died. As death begins to work its way out in Walter Donovan, the Templar Knight says simply, but profoundly, "He chose poorly."

Similarly, with respect to what God values, we chose poorly. And the consequences of that choice *continue* today. Death is our constant adversary. Disease is a consistent companion. Decay and destruction are seemingly permanently on display.

Therefore, our demand of God to deal with evil is a demand not to be held accountable for the evil *we* caused (and still cause today). Evil is winning and will continue to win until the Lamb returns for His own and restores the earth to its Eden-based heritage. God *is* loving and it is His love that continues to give us free will to either honor Him or denounce Him, to either embrace Him or call Him ineffective or to either bow to Him or dismiss Him from our lives.

Evil winning and God is loving are not mutually exclusive conditions. Because of our insistence He accepts our ideas on how to improve paradise, these two concepts exist simultaneously.

We cannot go back to Eden, but we can look forward to a "new heaven and a new earth" (Rev 21:1). In this place, "*He* will wipe away every tear from their eyes and death shall be no more, neither shall there be mourning, nor crying, nor pain anymore for the former things have passed away" (Rev 21:4).

Evil *will* lose. ""And the devil who had deceived them was thrown into the lake of fire and sulfur where the beast and the false prophet were, and they will be tormented day and night forever and ever" (Rev 20:10).

Our enemy, who convinced Adam and Eve to demand God give them a focus group *will* be done in, and done in forever. Paradise will be restored and given to all those whose names are recorded in the Book of Life.

Questions:

1) Which version of "evil winning" is most relevant to you, the micro or the macro? Why?

2) How does God speak to each of these in His word?

3) What has caused you to question if God really is loving?

4) What form of evil raises the question of there being a loving God the most? What can you do about it?

Chapter 9:

You need to heal and save the people I pray for

This is one of the hardest and most complex demands we have in our hearts.

This notion is usually born out of a deeply personal and an exquisitely painful emotional loss. Those in this place insist God clear His actions through them. And, typically, these are people with a pretty serious faith system in place. They *know* that God is a God of healing which means they are pretty comfortable handling the Bible and seeing the promises contained therein. They trust, in a sense, that God's will is fairly clear. He wants *no* one to perish. He told the disciples to "ask *anything* in My name and you will receive it." (John 15:7). Jesus doubles down on this concept when He chastises the disciples by saying, "You have not because you ask not." So, there is a solid amount of data these people *know* on how God "should work". And, they take Him up on the use of faith in requests to heal or save people they love and care about.

John Van Veen

A friend of mine was telling me about his journey of faith. He had
been very faithful in going to church, embracing the commands
in God's Word, and trying to be obedient in each arena of his
life. When his father was diagnosed with cancer, he *knew* to pray
for healing. Bring your petitions boldly to the throne of grace
(Heb 4:16). He lived that. He just knew God was going to heal his
dad. God had to. Doing so aligned with His words.

His father passed, rather quickly. My friend was completely undone
by God's lack of response to the many prayers of faith offered up
for healing. He got so upset at God that he stopped coming to
church, stopped reading his Bible, and stopped calling people to
repentance. He confessed that he really believed God owed him and
His payment would be healing of his beloved father. Thankfully,
he found God's perspective to be sufficient and he is, today, much
more confident in his place and more understanding of the Lord's
sovereignty and has become a critical leader in his church.

We were attending a church that routinely did "prayer and praise
services". The focus of these were to gather to pray over the issues
in one's life, whether they be emotional, relational, physical. And
interspersed with this prayer time was a "praise time" where people
could share a testimony about God's goodness, faithfulness, and
kindness. At one particular service, a person gets up and declares the
glories of God for healing his wife from cancer. He was so passionate,
so grateful, that more than a few people were moved to tears.

I was sitting near the back when a woman, tears streaming down
her face, got up and bolted for the exit. As an elder, I felt some
responsibility for her exit, so I followed her and found her sobbing
in the hallway.

"What's going on?" I asked.

Her answer floored me: "Why did God heal this man's wife and
allow my husband to die? I can't celebrate that. I'm too hurt."

When God doesn't provide the answer we think we need, we can put ourselves in the position where He no longer warrants my attention.

This is a conundrum that vexes many.

Why God heals some here on Earth and others only in Heaven remains profoundly perplexing. Certainly, healing seems like a good way to broadcast the wonder and glory of our God. Yet, He only heals a relatively small percentage, at least, that is what my experiences would tell me. Nonetheless, to insist God heal is a vastly different emotional posture than requesting God heal. The former sets our heart and will *against* God and the latter espouses humility and submission. The former predetermines how God must act and the latter yields to however God acts. The former says, "You need to consult with me before acting," and the latter says, as Mary did, "Behold I am a servant of the Lord, let it be to me according to your word." (Luke 1:38).

The reality that hits hard for us is: "God is not here to do our bidding."

We do not like that. Even as we understand it from a human parent-child relationship. We *know* that if all we did as parents was to cave to the child's demands, this child would grow up completely self-absorbed and incredibly unruly. There is a logical and legitimate need for the parent to *not* do the child's bidding.

Yet, in our relationship with God, we still do not like His refusal to do our bidding. Especially in times of great emotional distress, we want, nay, demand a God who will do our bidding. He needs to, because we instinctively know what is best for us. When God does not come to the table, does not invite us into a focus group on how to handle sickness, injury, accident, and death, many find Him detestable and walk away. God did not listen. He does not care.

Biblically, sickness, accidents, and death were never designed to be our lot. Eden was filled with life, goodness, care, and peace. It was our rebellion that brought all this upon us, our earth, and all future generations. We cannot undo it.

Yes, God is a God of the miraculous. Still to this day. But *we* are not the ones to demand which miracles God performs and which ones He should not. He does everything, the Bible tells us, for His glory. That He blesses one person or family with a miraculous healing in no way binds Him to do that for any other person or family.

Solomon wrote that God is the author of prosperity and calamity (Ecc 7:14). Both serve His purpose, as hard as that may seem to us especially if we seem to be the one under the weight of "calamity".

Sickness and disease remind us we are not forever in this physical, human state. These things inevitably lead to death, which the writer of Hebrews is set to happen to *every* human, *ever*. "It *is* appointed for man to die, then face judgment"(Heb 9:27). Death reminds us *we* have an appointment with Jesus *through* death, and it is at this time we will give account. It is in the accounting that makes death so fearful for so many, for they instinctively know they will come up short.

God uses these things that plague and bewilder us, that upset and distress us to point us to the reality of our frailty–our temporary standing. It is when these things come to our consciousness, we have to decide what we do with them. God says, "It is because of these things that I sent My Son to die, so that in Him, *you* will never have to taste eternal death." Sickness, disease, accidents, death all created by sin, but used by God to help us hunger for Him, and perhaps find Him for He is not far (Acts 17:28).

Questions:

1) Have you lost someone close to you? How did you see God in all of this?

2) Have you been seriously ill, or injured? How did you see God in all of this?

3) Where have you seen God overcome, do something the doctors said was "unlikely"? What was the impact on you?

4) How are you preparing for future tragic, traumatic, and taxing times?

Chapter 10:

If I give you more, what will You give me?

This chapter focuses on this instinctive tendency we seem to have of a Quid Pro Quo with God. You know that sense that goes like this: if I give God something, then He should give me something back. We have this sentiment at work in nearly all of our human relationships which means we tend to expect it to exist between God and me. So, this chapter, despite its heading is not solely about the "Prosperity Gospel" promise, the one that says, "If you give God $10 He will give you $100, because you can't outgive God."

Sure, it is not possible to outgive God. But the bigger issue in this sentiment is you believe God should *want* to negotiate the terms of life with you. Someone believing in this sentiment might see faith as not a matter of surrender, but of what I call "negotiated peace". And like most negotiations, they never put their best offer on the table *first*. They hold some things of value back in hopes that A) they won't need to give everything away, or, B) they have something of value to extract something else of value they need from the other party.

My first assignment with the company I mentioned in an earlier chapter that introduced me to "focus groups" was as manager of a production team. Not necessarily a tough assignment, but to be honest, made tougher because this was at a union plant. *Everything* was negotiated. *Every* work practice. *Every* rule of discipline. And, of course, *every* aspect of the compensation plan. *Everything* was negotiated. And this ran completely counter to my natural disposition to "wing it" on nearly everything I did. So, naturally, having to live by such a restrictive process really rubbed on me.

During my tenure at this site, I lived through two contract negotiations, meaning "here's the package management is prepared to offer," and the resultant reaction vote of the union to accept or reject that package of wages, benefits, and work rules.

Before the package was formally submitted, though, it was negotiated. The Department of Labor issued a decree that both parties must "negotiate in good faith". What this meant, in part, is that neither side could submit its *best* position upfront. No, there needed to be a sense of "I want this fringe benefit, so I'm prepared to give up this work rule to get it."

Negotiated terms. In this way, the theory goes, *both* sides will feel like they have won something or, sadly, that the other side lost something it valued.

Well, many in the faith think that is how our lives should work with God. "Yes, I believe in You, God, as my savior, but if you want me to be a good husband, You will have to give me something in exchange. Like changing my wife's offensive behavior. It is only right. I do this in nearly every other arena of my life, why should matters of faith be any different?" And thus, we insist God come to the table and negotiate the terms of our obedience. I give a little. He gives a little and together we find something that works for the both of us.

Jesus warned us that money will compete with Him for the place of greatest honor in our lives, so it is no wonder that one of the examples of negotiating with God comes from the area of surrendering our bank accounts to Him. Yes, *tithing*. This person wanted to give more to the church (I suspected it was because he needed a bigger tax write off, for he had a great year financially).

His question of me was, "If I give more to the church, what do you think God is likely to do for me?"

Speechless, I really had no reply. And yes, my suspicions were confirmed, sadly.

Our time and talent are also good places to look for an attitude that wants to negotiate with God.

A member of the church we were attending felt called to go to the mission field. He was deeply stressed by what this could mean to his way of life. He knew it would radically change given the part of the world he was feeling called to.

In despair, he said to me: "If God would assure me I'll be safe, I'll go."

While he had come to terms with the financial implications of the mission field, he could not do so for the health and safety aspects of the call to go to the harvest field. He wanted to negotiate with God on how he would surrender the use of his talents to go into missions. Safety seemed to be paramount versus surrendering it all to Him.

To be fair, I have fallen victim to this mindset as well.

When I finished my coursework, and got the associated "Certificate of Pastoral Ministry," God led me to the church I currently serve in. I was nearing the end of my first year of service, when a rather serious heart issue arose.

I was hospitalized and had what is now frequently deemed a *procedure*. It was life changing, to be sure. But part of what I had to wrestle with was how this procedure unmasked the "deal" I thought God and I had struck concerning taking on the role of Under-shepherd. I found resentment rising up in me for serving Him and He not protecting my health so I could serve Him. Without really consciously setting this in my thinking, it was clear that I did, in fact, try to negotiate with God about the implicit terms and conditions I had in my service to Him.

One final example. We were counseling another married couple, and the husband was being convicted of his heavy-handed dealings with his wife and children. Of course, this did not necessarily mean he agreed with why he was being confronted.

If he was heavy-handed, it was because "she was impossible to live with." In his mind, she would not let him be the leader of the house. But, as the Holy Spirit kept pressing the point of his surrender, he angrily asserted, "If *she* would submit to my authority, then I'll be more gentle."

Negotiating terms versus surrendering to His counsel.

Here is where it can hurt. God is *not* in the negotiation business. He is not trying to broker peace between warring factions, as an outsider. *He* is the offended party. *We* are the ones guilty of grave offenses toward Him. Therefore, as the one offended, He has every right to set the terms and conditions for *any* form of relationship with Him. Now, add to this the reality that He is the Creator and *we* are only the created, and we get a fuller picture of why surrender is the *only* option He will consider.

As World War II was nearing an end, the Allies presented the terms of surrender to the Japanese. They did not like them. The Japanese delegation offered a counter that let them hold onto some things. Though, because of the gross violation of American rights, the Allies stood firm.

"Complete, unconditional surrender or else..." Well, if the Americans were grossly violated, how do we think the Holy, pure, and sinless Creator was treated by His rebellious creation? Paul said we were "enemies, hostile in mind" toward God (Rom 5:10; 8:7). We hated Him, yet He provided a way to a relationship. However, that way is *solely*, completely, and only on His terms. Faith in the need for Jesus as our savior and Lord. Without this, we will continue to be at enmity with God even if we say we believe in Him. A heart that wants to negotiate is a heart that wants to stay at the table and demand God take its input.

Questions:

1) Where are you trying to negotiate with God? What subjects or areas of your life?

2) What would surrender look like?

3) How has God exposed what is really in your heart concerning His need to be the singular leader of your life?

4) How are you trying to convince God you have something He needs?

Chapter 11:

I wouldn't do it that way, so God can't either

This particular approach to demanding God invite us to a focus group is one of the more interesting ones, to me. It comes from a place of arrogance. I know, that sounds harsh. Yet the premise is that *our* intentions, our reactions to things, our design for a perfect life, and our thoughts on a desirable world to abide in is that we, and only we, know how best to accomplish. Therefore, when God steps out of *our* definitions of right, fair, decent, loving, hateful, etc., we call Him to account.

When we accuse God. When we angrily ask, "What are You *doing?*" This is as much a charge we bring against Him. It becomes our indictment of Him because what is going on, or not going on, in the areas of living that impacts us most directly.

But none of this is new. The theologian, Francois Voltaire, quipped centuries ago (sometime early in the eighteenth century), "God made man in His own image and man returned the favor."

His point is a familiar one. Mankind keeps insisting that this external force that, at the time of Voltaire's writing, was generally agreed to have created the world and all of mankind, was somehow limited and needed help to get His life "in order". He certainly *needs* us to help Him direct all that He created. He needs a focus group on all of this. And in our insistence to this shared design and operation of creation, we force "God" to think, act, and react as we would.

In practice, this thesis goes like this: If we wouldn't do it, then God shouldn't. And conversely if we would do it, then we expect God to do so. Anything less than this would be sinful on God's part.

One of the axioms I have heard numerously that reflect this view of "God" is, "God wants me to be happy." We want to be happy. Everyone wants to be happy. *Therefore*, this "god" I have created in my own image also wants me to be happy. And then such folks set out on a life designed by themselves to find happiness, at sometimes extreme cost, assured in the blessing of their "god".

A couple of examples come to mind. I was a newly elected elder to a rapidly growing church. The founding pastor had stepped aside to pursue a career in counseling. The new pastor was extremely dynamic and clearly had the gift of evangelism. The church was seeing unparalleled growth. During all of this, the founding pastor and his family continued to attend this church.

One day a call came in. The founding pastor and his wife wanted to meet with the elder board. At this meeting, the wife confessed to having an affair. Of course, after the shock wore off, the questions of repentance and reconciliation were posited. Her response was my first educational moment in this demand that God be exactly like "me".

She told us: "I've never felt closer to God than when I am with the other man, and I know that I'm happy with God on this account."

Stunned, I had no idea what to say. This was a very new experience, thinking, up to this point, that such flagrant sin, when uncovered, would automatically engender brokenness. I guess I was expecting a sorrow like we saw from David when Nathan confronted him over his sin with Bathsheba (2 Sam 12).

Clearly, she exhibited none of this. As I was wrestling with a response, the new pastor said something incredibly profound, "Just because you are happy with God does not mean He is happy with you." *My, was that wisdom.* It hit at the heart of this demand that God be "like me" with power and truth.

Many years later, my wife and I found ourselves counseling a couple in a marriage crisis. He wanted to leave his spouse. Raising children, to him, was a drag on his time, his freedom, and his style. He had had enough. Sure, he played the "I'm-in-counseling-game" for a few years. But her repeated insistences that they, as a couple, keep engaging counsel finally unmasked him. In exasperation he declared, "I know God wants me happy, and I'm not happy here, so I am going to leave."

There are other ways this demand that God be like me expresses itself. The concept of "fair or unfair" is often simply a demand of God for a focus group can be witnessed. We see our circumstances in the context of "fair or unfair" and as a wise sage once said, "We claim life is unfair when something horrible hits, but we never think that it was 'unfair' that we got a huge blessing."

We look at life through the lens of our beliefs, experiences, and expectations and use those as the measure of what is fair or unfair. Then, we insist God hold the same measure we do.

A member in my church had just lost his wife of nearly 30 years. He married late in life, so he was well into his late 50s when she passed. Not at all unusual, his grief was profound. In our times together I tried to remind him that grieving was natural, good, and a process that God ordained. He had time to work through this profound sense of loss.

He stopped coming to see me and gradually stopped coming to church. I went to his house and we talked. "Unfair" was the summation of his rant.

He had lost his mother two years previous and his dad four years previous. And all he could muster, in between the deep sobs, was "it is so unfair. I have lost so much. No one else has had to live with what I have been forced to endure. It is *unfair*." He blamed God, of course, for not seeing life his way and therefore, by not consulting him on what a "fair" life would be.

There are so many more examples of this type of conviction, that God *must* see life the way I do and must therefore endorse my view of how it should be managed. We demand He do so...

Of course, the biblical revelations declare a vastly different perspective. As Isaiah was encouraged to write, "My ways are higher than your ways and as the heavens are above the earth so are My thoughts above your thoughts" (Is 55:9). In the 38 chapters of Job where God is silent, we see the musings, the frustration and the angst of an extremely righteous man and his erstwhile friends. If anyone had any right to demand God explain Himself, it was Job. He could, unlike the vast majority of *us*, find *no sin* in his life that would warrant any discipline more or less the exquisitely punishing discipline he was enduring.

Finally, when God had heard enough, notice what He does *not* say in Chapters 38-40. He does not say, "Well done, My son. I *told* Satan you wouldn't cave and you *didn't*. I am *so* proud of you!!"

No. God does not credit Job with any such performance successes through this dark season of the soul. Rather, He reinforces His position as God, sovereign and supreme. "Where were you when

I laid the foundations of the earth?" (Job 38:4). And from this question, the Lord goes on a nearly 100 verse defense of His authority to lead not just the universe in general, but each person in specific.

Of pertinence to the issue of fair and unfair, God asks of Job, "Would you discredit My justice? Would you condemn Me to justify yourself?" (Job 40:8). That is at the core of the issue in this "God, you must be like me" demand. We want to justify ourselves even knowing that doing so condemns the holy God of creation. Of course, even as much as we want this to happen, God insists even more that it not only cannot exist, it will not exist.

Job ends his book with the admission of humility that God seeks in all of us. Rather than insist He be and do as we would "be and do", Job concludes with, "You asked, 'Who is this that obscures My counsel without knowledge?' Surely, I spoke of things I did not understand, things too wonderful for me to know" (Job 42:3).

Job gets it. We all want God to be "like us", but the reality is, if He were, we would have a God who speaks without knowledge, and speaks without understanding. *We* are the limited creature. He is the holy, sovereign, almighty Creator. Blessed are those that live with such assurance and conviction.

Questions:

1) Have you ever uttered the "I *know* God wants me to be happy" sentiment? Where do you find biblical support for that? What is it He truly wants for you?

2) Have you ever demanded that God make "fair" what you found "unfair"? What did you learn through that experience?

3) How have you been like Job trying to give God counsel?

4) What does the holiness of God demand of you?

Chapter 12:

We want God to partner with us

This is a tricky one and it comes in many forms. The essence of this demand that God invite us in to reshape His faith process is a belief that we have earned an "equal say" in what is required in our life. This is true whether we are talking salvation or we are talking sanctification. This is about us believing that the best solution for our lives is if "God and I hammer out a peaceful coexistence."

One of the more popular ways this is expressed is in this oft-used phrase, "I'm going to do (fill in the blank) *for* Jesus."

The speaker typically puts very pious sounding things to "fill in that blank". I'm going to work for Jesus. I'm going to go to the mission field for Jesus. I'm going to get sober for Jesus. I'm going to... you get the idea, do something noble *for* Jesus. It conveys the notion that without our help Jesus would go wanting, that some key activity would not get done or some necessary advancement of His kingdom hangs in the balance. He *needs me* is the underlying belief.

Our church routinely supported various faith-based addiction recovery programs. This is right to do. Faith-based addiction recovery programs typically show a much lower recidivism rate than non-faith based. There is power and healing in Christ. I want to be "on record" in complete support of these types of addiction recovery programs.

Yet, over the years of being involved in these programs, one of the common themes from the graduating class was saturated with what the graduate was going to do *for* Jesus. Now, I know, some of you are going to say, "Well, this is only good. They want to repay Jesus for getting them through this program." And that is exactly my point. We cannot repay Jesus. We can only surrender.

To repay is to say, "I've earned my seat at Your table." To repay is to say, "We are now equals. You did this for me, and now I've returned the favor. We are, therefore, partners now." And many of the graduates who tried to repay Jesus found, sadly, over time, that they once again needed His grace and mercy in their fight against addiction.

Another way this belief that God should partner with us comes is in the pursuit of the big things in life we are convinced we *need*. And much of this comes from those who are spiritually apprised. The language of this group goes like this, "Well, God told me He wanted me to have this job." Or, "Well, I heard from God that this is the person I am to marry." I call this using the "God card" to ensure *no one* questions you, your decisions, and your motivations. When I am a bit more cynical, I will say, "They are 'blaming God' for their pursuit of their wants and desires."

We had a couple in our small group home Bible study many years back. He was from another State but met his wife in the city where we lived. He was young and aggressive in his career. He had wanted to go home for this great new job opportunity. His wife was not so much resisting, as she was questioning the need to move. They had a young family and she had begun to make close friends where they were currently living as well.

Our group, sensing the tension on this issue, decided we would allocate some of the group time one evening to this topic. "Oh, I have heard from God that He wants us to move. We have a chance to work in a new neighborhood and share the gospel." It was hard to argue with his passion.

Within six months they were gone.

About eighteen months after they moved to, erstwhile, obey the voice of God on this job opportunity, they all came back to the area we lived for a vacation. Because she felt connected to our small group, they popped in during our meeting time. Because this was about 18 months after they moved away, "How's it going" had to be the first question we asked of them. With eyes downcast and a soft voice, he said, "I was the one who really wanted to leave, but I knew she would not support it outright, so I convinced her I had heard from God. I lied. It was all me. And now, I am miserable. The job could not be worse. We should have never moved." Playing the "God card" had kept all those who loved them at bay. Sadly.

In many situations we have encountered while counseling couples, we run across people who either in their grief or in despair will turn quickly to try to find another soul mate. Often to the chagrin of other loved ones.

Part of our process is to ask how this pursuit of another soul mate is perceived by family and friends. In situations where family and friends have been deeply concerned and have pushed back on the plans to embrace a new soul mate, we have seen the "God card" get played again.

"We both heard from God that this was right to do," came the reply to the push back, so they pressed on anyway. Should they have? As all involved claimed to be in Christ, the division and hurt this caused suggested they were not operating in a spirit of unity.

"Blaming" God for their desires has created a schism in the family circle that may never be repaired. A clear indicator that something is very untoward in this situation (James 4:1–3).

That is us wanting what we know may not be right for us, at least not right at that time. This is us so insistent on gaining this thing, fearing opposition to our want, we pull out the God-said card and try to bully people into silence, if not shame them into outright agreement.

When we do this, we not only misrepresent our real motivations, we over-spiritualize them. We, in essence, put ourselves as "equals" with God. The message we try to forcefully send is this: "He and I consult in ways you clearly don't. Therefore, you are not capable of understanding why my way is not only right, it is blessed by my partner, God Himself." "God said" is typically enough to ensure I get what I want with the least resistance possible.

The difference between "God said" and truly "hearing" from God is in the impact on those around. When we are trying to manipulate God, or manipulate others, or play on the faith others have in Christ, it usually ends up bad either in the long-term, or in increasingly dysfunctional, and breaking of, relationships.

When one truly "hears from God," there is humility and, as I've experienced, a genuine willingness to openly discuss and help others work through their fears tied to what another may have heard. There is no rush, just the joyful fruit of the Spirit at work in all those involved. Evidence of the kind of unity Paul encouraged the Philippian church to intentionally put into practice (Phil 2).

Finally, and perhaps in no other area of our lives do we *insist* God bring us to the table and get our input more than when it involves our physical well-being, our health. Being a pastor brings one into many difficult and emotionally taxing situations. Certainly, the death of a loved one being the most taxing. A close second would be receiving the news of a serious health diagnosis. Cancer, heart, and kidney issues seem to be the worst, for they all portend an increasingly debilitating disease rendering life more and more painful, more and more difficult.

It is not at all uncommon for me, as a pastor, to hear language such as, "How did this happen? I did everything I was supposed to." Or, "What did I do to deserve this?" Or, "Why did God put me here (in this place of physical death)?" The passion, confusion, and angst are palpable. The message I receive from these people is one of why didn't God protect me, after all I have done for Him? In other words, God did not consult with me, He did not value me, and He certainly was not interested in what was best for me. Why didn't He listen? I thought we were partners!

This is an area where we most often forcefully insist we be involved in God's plans. Few respond to such crises with grace and humility. Some with deep hurt. Some with bewilderment and some with anger at the prospect of losing one's life to a horrible illness or injury. To surrender all, we must, well, surrender all. And for most of us, surrendering our physical existence is the single greatest challenge in our walk of faith. COVID 19 drove that point home quite clearly.

Yet, there are stellar examples of how to surrender well. Our friend had received a horrible diagnosis. She had been battling cancer for about 18 months when the doctor told her she now had Free Cell cancer, which is nearly impossible to beat. She tried treatments but found them to be so debilitating that it left her without *any* energy, more or less a passion to live.

As she was battling during her last days, her daughter came into her room and read her the last four chapters of the Book of Psalms. When she had finished, she looked at her mom, completely beaten by this brutal enemy, and said, "Mom, I have no idea why I was led to read these verses to you."

Without skipping a beat, in a whisper of a voice, her mom firmly stated, "Praise God, always. No excuses."

Within five days, she passed. Surrendered. Trusting God to be the loving sovereign God He is, who did not need her help in determining what was best for her. She had no intention of demanding God invite her to a focus group on how to deal with her deeply lamentable physical realities.

The fundamental questions in all of this are: Does God need us to partner with Him? Does He speak so that division and strife are the expected outcome? Well, the first question is easier. *No*, He does not need a partner. God, the Father, in calling us His children, gives us special privileges including being joint heirs with *Jesus*. In that way, we are equal. All the riches of His heaven are equally available to us.

But, without any doubt, His ways, His thoughts are *not* ours. *We* cannot be trusted to produce holiness. Only the Holy Spirit can. *We* cannot be depended upon to establish righteousness. Only Jesus was able to do that. We cannot be the determiner of the way to the Father. Only Jesus is capable of doing that. Our sinful nature profoundly stains *everything* about what we do, think, and act. Therefore, to suggest that Jesus needs us to partner with Him to get His objectives for us achieved is simply sinful thinking.

This is *His* world. He owns the cattle on every hill. He hung the moon, the sun, and every star. He is the wisdom of all ages. His is preeminent and immanent. He is above all and in all. He is, though, very willing to share His glory with us. He is very willing to include us as vehicles to deliver His heart and truth to the world around us. He is very willing to call us "son", to call us "daughter". He is even very willing to share His inheritance with us.

Make no mistake, however. He is *not* willing to call us "partners" with equal say in the direction of His plans. Faith in Him declares we will trust Him, in His character, in His promises, in His Word. This demands we live with assurance in the things hoped for and conviction in the things not seen. For much of His desires for us are not yet understood, not yet seen. The magnificence of Heaven, *He* understands and therefore can rightly value. We have little to no clue on the glories that await. Paul said it was a weight of glory that we cannot comprehend. Living with conviction in the certainty of a life with Him in glory translates to "yes, should I walk through the valley of the shadow of death, I will fear nothing for *You* are with me *You* comfort me..." (Psalm 23:4–6)

Now, to get at the second question. "Does He speak so that division and strife are the expected outcome?" Jesus declared "if you don't hate mother, father, sister, and brother you are not worthy of the kingdom of heaven." (Matt 10:37). Jesus said He came to set family members against family members. He came not to bring peace, but division (Luke 12:51). So, one considers these verses and might conclude that division is not simply OK, but necessary.

But context is always vital to proper interpretation of Scripture. In the verses cited above, Jesus was talking about the division that occurs within family units because some believe, and some do not. That His presence would cause many to be angry and want to hurt those that receive Him and begin living as a child of His kingdom.

The message for the family of faith is much different. *Unity* is His theme which He developed while ministering to the disciples and so poignantly shared in John 17. These disciples then, like Paul, carried this out in their writings. *One* good example of this is Paul in Phil 2. James went so far as to say if there is division *among* those in Christ, then someone is clearly being self-centered, selfish and, consequently, sinning.

So, while division can occur within the body of Christ, the vast majority of the time it is due to one party *not* getting what they are lusting after and then resisting coaching as to the sinfulness of their desires. In the end, the message is the same. God does not need our help. He has got this *if* we can learn to be "still and experience that He is God."

Questions:

1) When has someone used the "God-said" card on you? How did you feel? What were the long-term results of the action "God said" they could or should take?

2) Have you ever tried to sway someone by "dropping the God card" on another? What was going on inside you at that moment?

3) In what area(s) of your life are you more prone to demand God invite you to the table to "discuss" what is best for you?

4) What is the fruit of the Spirit that best tells you that all is well, even when circumstances are suggesting it is not well?

Chapter 13:

"But we VOTED"

This can be a long discussion or a short one, for the point seems obvious.

I was a recent convert to the cross of Jesus Christ. This would have been in the early 1980s when I heard John MacArthur make a very provocative statement. It went something like this, "The church is only 20 years behind society." His point was while the "church" rails against the rise of what would soon become a societal norm, in 20 years the "church" would, in fact, embrace the very norm it railed against. At the time, I was too new to the faith to appreciate the prophetic wisdom of MacArthur's statement.

Fast forward 40 years, and yes, my experience would say what MacArthur said has, by and large, played itself out. And from this process we get this "demand" of God to invite us to the table and speak into *His* area of authority. "But God, *we* voted, and *we* think this is a better way."

The issue, at the time, if I remember correctly, was the role of women in leadership of His church. There was much debate, at the time. I was on the elder board of a rapidly growing conservative evangelical church. Within a period of five years, I was part of leadership teams (comprised of both women and men) that had studied this topic three different times at two different churches.

GOD DOESN'T DO FOCUS GROUPS

Using whatever resources were available, searching the Scriptures and desperately praying, the leadership concluded each time that the Bible speaks to men being in the key leadership positions: elder, pastor, and shepherd.

Certainly, society saw this as repressive. Some even within the church accused us of being out of touch. We were called misogynists, archaic, prideful. It was a hard period. And by the early twenty-first century, women were very common in leadership positions within the church, as elder, as pastor, as shepherd, including the two churches where I participated in the search of Scripture over the qualifications of biblical leadership

Why? "We voted. We looked and saw the great potential of women in society and thought that was right for the church, too. It keeps us relevant."

By the late 1990s and into the early 2000s, the issue the church railed against was homosexuality. Whereas one had to dig through Scripture to a penetrating degree to reach a conclusion concerning women in leadership, the Bible is very clear that those who are active in the practice of sinful lifestyles, be that adultery, drunkenness, or homosexual practices, even if active within the church, are disqualified from leading. So, the church railed against the societal norm that homosexuality was not a choice, but a genetic disposition.

Fast forward twenty years and sure enough, to MacArthur's point, many denominations and churches have now voted and declared that a practicing homosexual can and should be an elder, a pastor, and a shepherd.

Why? "We voted and, God, this helps You stay relevant in our world. We are just helping you advance and change."

Somewhere we believe that if we vote, God must honor it. We "force" Him to honor our vote by establishing the democratic decision-making process as the new standard of leadership, and as the new method of how we discern holiness and righteousness.

As we discussed in Chapter 7, the Barna-led survey reaffirms the power we believe we have because we "voted on it." There *is* more than one way to heaven–we decided. After all, God blessed us with democracy, and He needs to honor the results of our votes.

We forget, of course, that God doesn't do focus groups. He is *not* a democratically elected leader. He is God Almighty, King of all kings, President of all presidents, and God Sovereign who needs *nothing from* us.

We kind of accept all this about Him, this "Higher Power" most will ascribe exists. Yet, the struggle is exquisitely intense within us that we do not get a vote as to what is "right, acceptable" and thereby what is "wrong and unacceptable." Consequently, we *push* on Him to accept our understanding, our collective wisdom, the outcome of our democracy-infused vote which impacts even many fundamentally conservative churches across the world even today.

Paul addressed this process in Romans 1. In verse 21, Paul tells us that "although they knew God (i.e., willing to acknowledge there is a "higher power" as we would say) they did not honor Him as God or give thanks to Him, but they became futile in their thinking and their foolish hearts were darkened." We want to vote on it, but God said the best thing you can do is *honor him*. The increasing refusal to do so leads to the very thing we see play out over the years, namely, "became futile in thinking".

In our futility we insist God embrace our wisdom. Paul concludes in verse 32 with, "Though they knew God's decree (i.e., we *know* what the Bible says, what He insists be *the* way to live) that those who practice such things (i.e., envy, murder, gossip, heartlessness, etc.—see verses 29–31 for the complete list) deserve to die, they not only do them, but give approval to those who practice them." That is, "We *voted* and *we* decided the things God opposes are, in fact, deemed good and right."

Instead of taking David's posture, namely, "Who is man that You should take notice of him" (Psalm 8:4). We take the defiant posture and "approve" things He clearly says is not in our best interest.

"There is a way that seems right to man, but the end thereof is death" (Prov 14:12). What is in our best interest is to live as our Creator deemed correct. If we agree He made us, that would say *He* knows how His creation functions best. He knows how to fix it when it breaks. He knows what is needed to function at the top of our potential. He has given us an Owner's Manual that lays this all out.

Like Henry Ford and his famous Model T, God has written an "owner's manual" to help us achieve "our best life now"…and for eternity. Even as we would never think of using an owner's manual from a Chevrolet to fix the problem we are having with our Mercedes Benz, so, too, we should never think to use human wisdom to fix the problem we are having with our soul. God gave us the right manual to use and if used it will lead to rest, peace, assurance, contentment, and eternal salvation.

Questions:

1) What issues of society do you see as "right" for the "church of Jesus" to embrace? Why?

2) How often have you dug into Scripture yourself to find "the answer" to an issue laid before the church? If not "always", why not?

3) Have you participated in a vote that changed how your church "saw" an issue? How did that work out? More peace within, or more division? What might that tell you?

4) What will it take to cling to God's word and keep the church not 20 years behind society, but 2,000?

Chapter 14:

Why It is in OUR Best Interest that God does NOT do focus groups

As many and varied the reasons that drive us to want God to invite us to a focus group, as have been shared in these previous chapters. As passionate and urgent the reasons we feel we have that would force God to the table to engage us in a focus group. Let me be clear *It is in our best interest that God forgoes our demands for input* to reshape what faith and success as a person of faith looks like. I know, that sounds counterintuitive. So, let's take a look at it.

There are many verses that tell us of His steadfastness in both His character and in His commands of us. The writer of Hebrews gives us many passages about the superior nature of Jesus, but for these purposes, there are two that are particularly relevant and, therefore, deserve attention. The first is Heb 13:8 where the author states, "Jesus Christ is the same yesterday and today and forever!" Said differently, Jesus is *not* ever changing, growing, maturing like we humans must. He does not evolve. His value system is not being updated by all that occurs around Him. He does not gain a new perspective because of what He's experienced over successive generations of time.

No, what He laid out for His disciples, what His Spirit laid out for the writers of the New Testament is *exactly* what He lays out for us, today and for every generation to come until His glorious return. Nothing different. No varying expectations. No modifications to the journey of sanctification that is required of all those who believe in Him.

In addition, the author of Hebrews opens up his book with a powerful truth. Heb 1:1–2,"Long ago, at many times and many ways God spoke to our fathers by the prophets, but in these last days He has spoken to us by His Son..." These "last days" are the days *we* live in, and every generation will live in until the fullness of the time is complete, and He returns.

Note in this, *no one* else is appointed as the voice of God. No one else has the information and access to what *we* need to be productive and mature in our faith *save Jesus*. No one else can reveal truth that is essential for our spiritual development unless it aligns with the words of Jesus. This truth is a cornerstone truth of saving faith.

But *imagine* if these things concerning Jesus were *not* true, namely that He was not the same "yesterday, today, and forever," and that He is not the final messenger-voice of God to His children. Imagine, then, if God did in fact take input, if He agreed with those suggesting changes to "improve" the efficacy of His religion. Imagine God intentionally conducting a focus group on how to make His religion fit better with its users! What would this do to our faith? Our confidence? Our assurance and conviction? And most importantly, what might this do to our salvation?

So, let's tackle the assertion laid before us in Heb 1:1–2. If Jesus were not the final voice from God, how would that change the way we live by faith?

Practically, this would mean somewhere, some time along the flow of history, someone else would have a responsibility to give us the "new" and updated counsel from God. Like we get an update to the software on our phones. Perhaps this would happen once for every generation, or, for sake of ease of understanding, once a century, on the first day of that century. The latter makes it a bit easier for us to contemplate and see the implications.

As the year 2000 approached, for example, and we had been waiting for the latest word from God, what would we do? Would we lay aside some of His previous commands in anticipation of Him changing them, negating them or replacing them altogether? Would we put a hold on our spiritual lives, and its disciplines, because something new was about to be unveiled?

When the "word" finally comes on Jan 1, 2000, what does that do to all who lived under the "word" that came Jan 1, 1900, especially those that died during the intervening years? Does the new "word" invalidate the previous "word"? Does it merely "build on it" and give those now living MORE to do in their journey of faith or different things to do to show you do have saving faith? Would it include a "grandfather clause" that exempts all who died from having to achieve the standards in the updated version?

Who would be the chosen messenger-voice who would deliver this "new insight"? Who would God choose to bring the "new requirements" forward? Given the goofiness of those claiming to speak for God when He *is* the same yesterday, today, and forever, can you fathom how that information "void" would attempt to be filled if He did provide "updates"? We would have *so* many people speak up claiming to be speaking for God. Deception, manipulation, and falseness would be rampant, but how would *we* who love the

Lord *know* who is a false prophet when the message from the Lord keeps changing?

With Jesus the same yesterday, today, and forever, we can easily run to His Word and test the message from these would-be "voices of God". We are told to "test the Spirits" (1 John 4:1) which we can only because Jesus is the same yesterday today and forever.

The messages He got from His Father are what He shared openly with us (John 8:28). But how could we be that sure if God kept updating the "manual" based on "user input"? How could we live with confidence in the reality of our salvation and with conviction over the journey of sanctification?

Think about how you would "live by faith" under the condition that God did, in fact, do focus groups. The ever-changing landscape of His expectations would make trusting Him impossible. In addition, which version of His Word, then, must you hold as valid in making your decisions? We *might* get some things right, but most of the time we would be exasperated because the rules keep changing, the goals keep changing and the endpoint of our faith keeps changing. Nothing is more difficult, more demoralizing than "shooting at a moving target".

This would be akin to lining up for a 10,000-meter run. Everyone is at the start, but the course you are to run has not been told, nor is marked out on the street or trail you are running. Compounding this, no one is at the corners where you are supposed to be turning and a map showing the course has not been produced. Then, the gun goes off. Everyone starts to move, but in what direction? Everyone steps out without knowing how to successfully navigate the course to get to the finish line. If most did not walk off the course in disgust, *none* of them would return to "run" this event in the following year. Having God continue to speak and modify His expectations would be like this race, maddening and frustrating, leaving us no desire to continue in "it".

Finally, and hopefully without belaboring this critical point, if God did do focus groups, who decides who gets invited to His conference room? And then, what do you do if you *don't* get invited? You are still "stuck" with someone else's definition of what a "good" religion consists of. So, you may say, let *everyone* get a voice. God has to invite *everyone*. OK, let us assume that does happen. Now, again, who decides what the change God must make is going to be? Majority vote? Then what of those who hold the minority stake? Does their input get ignored? If so, then how are they to live in peace and rest knowing how they believe salvation and sanctification must be worked out is not being implemented?

Now, for the ultimate fear should God choose to engage us in focus groups. What happens if a focus group session two hundred years from now *changes* what is, in fact, the unpardonable sin, a sin for which you *know* you were guilty. Does this mean you get expelled from Heaven as soon as God adopts the input of this new group?

As has been laid out, these are but some of perhaps many more issues with profound impacts on eternity if God would choose to do focus groups. We would be in great despair and faith would be non-existent.

Therefore, let us truly honestly reflect on the *great* benefits we get because God does *not* do focus groups around His processes of salvation and sanctification. He knows better than to entrust Himself to man (John 2:24, 25). God is sovereign and blessed are those who can truly rest in His benevolent involvement with us.

Questions:

1) How have you demanded that God include you in a focus group? What would have been the outcome had He?

2) In what ways have you benefited from His "stubborn adherence to His plan"?

3) What confidence do you get from Jesus being the same yesterday, today and for as far into the future as we can see?

4) How can you now celebrate His refusal to seek input into how matters of faith are handled?

Chapter 15

Summary

Where do we get the idea that God, Himself, doesn't do focus groups to make His religion more appealing? Well, the first real hint at this reality comes in Deuteronomy 28. The people, finally done wandering the desert, are facing the Promised Land for the second time. This time they have the resolve to step across the Jordan and face those that possess the land. As Moses prepares them for this incredible step of faith, he recounts for them God's dealings with Israel, restates the Ten Commandments, and gives them other laws on how they are to live in a manner that God designed in relationship to Him and with one another.

When we get to Chapter 28, Moses is about done with all the preliminaries. It is in this chapter that Moses lays out for God's chosen people the choice they have obedience or disobedience. A choice He continues to give us today. Per God's own instruction, Moses tells the people in verses 1-14 all the glories that await them if they choose obedience. In verses 15-68, God lays out all the indicators that His people are choosing disobedience.

If there was *ever* a time for God to say, "Hey, try this new stuff out and if it doesn't work, we'll reshape it for you," *now* was it? His people getting ready to self-rule in *their* home, for the very first time, *this* would have been the ideal time for God to give them an alternate path to Him *if* they found what He was asking to be too hard, too wearisome, too out of touch, and too demanding. Having watched the previous generation fail so badly at honoring His expectations, now would have been the perfect time to change some things for this new generation, to give them a better chance at pleasing God.

Instead, God lays out serious consequences for *not* doing *exactly* as He commanded all generations of Israelites. *Serious* consequences. Verses 58 and 59 seem as good a summary as any to give us all an idea that He doesn't do focus groups. "If you are not careful to do *all* the words of this law that are written in this book, that you may fear this glorious and awesome Name, The Lord your God, *then* the Lord will bring on you and your offspring extraordinary afflictions, afflictions severe and lasting and sicknesses, grievous and lasting." Absolutely *no* hint that He wanted to renegotiate His process for life *in* Him under any circumstance or struggle.

There are many such passages in the Old Testament, especially in the Prophets who were speaking for God and repeatedly calling Israel back to obedience. Again, if God had any desire to modify His demands, He had plenty of opportunities to do so. Similar to the nation gathered on the east shore of the Jordan, if there was a time when God *could* have said, "Hey, let's rethink and retool My conditions for our relationship," coming back from exile would have given Him another *solid*, rational place to do so.

He *could* have said, "Man, I see your inability to keep My commandments ended up with you paying such an extreme price lots of deaths, the humiliation of deportation and the deep scars of being in exile. So, now that I am bringing you back to the Promised Land, how about if I ease up some on the demands so we don't have to go through such horrors again?"

We see in Nehemiah chapters 9 and 10 the progression of the exiles, now, finally back in the Promised Land. Seventy years they spent in captivity. Seventy years that Jeremiah foretold. With them returned, now would have been another ideal time for God to "tone it down a bit" to help His children "succeed" in pleasing Him. But, notice, after confessing the legacy of sin against God's character and His Word in Chapter 9, Nehemiah has the leadership sign a covenant with God. This covenant did *not* include one single modification to the standard to which Israel was initially called to live back when they were first called to cross the Jordan River. Not one.

Notice, Chapter 10, verses 28 and 29: "The rest of the people and all who separated themselves from the peoples of the lands to the Law of God all who have knowledge and understanding, join with their brothers, their nobles and enter into a curse and an oath to walk in God's law that was given to Moses and to observe and do all the commandments of the Lord our Lord and His rules and statutes."

There it is again. God is insisting on a relationship completely on His terms, no modifications, no input needed. He created us. He has the right to tell us how we are to function.

Certainly, though, you might argue, all of the above, while accurate, is still a reflection of the *old* covenant. Couldn't God, when He instituted the new covenant have modified the process and, in that, lowered the standard? Isn't it all about *grace* now? So, don't we get some input into how we all get along with God?

Well, let us start with Matt 22:34–39. Jesus is in Jerusalem for the final time. His passion is about three days away. He is in the courtyard of the temple once again parrying with the religious elite, who have tried for three years to catch Him doing something, anything, so they can justify their murderous desires.

In this particular exchange, captured by Matthew, a "lawyer, asked Him a question, to test Him. 'Teacher, which is the greatest commandment in the Law?'"

What a *perfect* chance for Jesus to share the updated version of God's expectations. What a great chance to say, "Heck, yes, the Father and I have abolished two of the commandments outright, modified four more to reduce their exclusivity. Therefore, there are really only four you now have to get really right. We looked at how *your* fathers' struggle with obedience to Our initial set of commandments. Therefore, My Father and I thought it best to take your struggles into account and go ahead and modify our demands."

Perfect time to share that the "Big Guy" upstairs heard all the complaining, all the calls for a focus group so our ideas and inputs could be embedded and stated in the *new* standard. If there was to be something "new", answering the lawyer's question would have been an *ideal* time for Jesus to download these new system requirements.

What did Jesus say? Verses 37-39: "You shall love the Lord your God with all your heart and with all your soul and with all your mind. This is the great and first commandment."

OK Got it. That is a pretty big commandment. I can understand why He would not want to mess with that. But, surely, *change* is coming, based on *our* inabilities and our input, right? Let us continue to read what Jesus answered. "And a second is like it. You shall love your neighbor as yourself. On these two commandments depend all the Law and the Prophets."

Did you read that? Jesus, in this second commandment basically said *all* the Law is *still* in play. *How* you satisfy them may have changed, *but* to satisfy them, you *must*. No changes. No lowering of the bar. No focus group input-driven by what the users say is needed to make it better. No, Jesus is holding the same standard His Father gave to Moses many centuries previous.

Finally, a quick trip to Revelation. This book is about the end of the Church Age, the end, really, of life as we know it. It sets up Jesus as *the* ruler of all and the One to be celebrated above all. From this perspective, we see the angel tell John in Rev 21:9, "You must not do that (i.e., worship the angel). I am just a fellow servant with you and your brothers the prophets and with those *who keep the words of this book*. Worship God."

As the end comes, John is completely overwhelmed with the majesty, the breadth, and the perfection of what is to come. He wants to worship the message, while the angel corrects him and says, "Worship the *message's author*," and the angel then aligns himself with John as simply a servant.

The angel also aligns himself with the prophets, those who spoke of the coming Christ and His rule. Those who consistently called Israel back to living out faith in the commandments God set before them.

Finally, the angel aligns himself with "those who keep the words of this book."

That is *us*, those who believe in Jesus and because of that *keep* the words of this book. In context of our scope, this means Jesus did not ever lower the standard. He did not ever seek input to find a way to make believing more convenient or easier. Rather, His expectations remain unchanged *keep the words of this book* as it was given for every generation since the law was given to Moses.

Obey Me. Honor Me. Submit to Me. That is the final message we get from Heaven when this age closes.

God doesn't do focus groups. He has clearly stated His standard. He has repeatedly reinforced that this *is* the standard. He has upheld its integrity from Day 1 to Day 0. We satisfy that only by faith working itself out in loving obedience to His standard. No shortcuts. No modifications. No change-ups, no matter how appealing these things may *seem* to us. God doesn't do focus groups.

The many ways man has tried to enlist God into allowing focus group events were enumerated. From the path to Heaven being too exclusive, to being a good person and everything in between. We have seen how our reactions to various situations that confront us truly are expressions that we firmly believe God needs to get our input, and *change* His standards, His expectations of us, if it comes to that. That would make our life easier for a moment but, as we saw, eternally unsettled, hopelessly restless.

God doesn't do focus groups and this truth is one of His great blessings and gifts to His people! May you find the joy and freedom of this truth.

CPSIA information can be obtained
at www.ICGtesting.com
Printed in the USA
LVHW041018110621
689906LV00005B/494